TEAM SPIRIT®

SMART BOOKS FOR YOUNG FANS

THE CLEVELAND INDIANS

BY

MARK STEWART

NORWOODHOUSE PRESS

CHICAGO, ILLINOIS

Norwood House Press
P.O. Box 316598
Chicago, Illinois 60631

For information regarding Norwood House Press, please visit our website at:
www.norwoodhousepress.com or call 866-565-2900.

All photos courtesy of Getty Images except the following:
Tom DiPace (4, 14, 23), Author's Collection (6, 16, 39, 42 bottom, 43 bottom right), Wilson Franks (7),
Black Book Partners Archives (9, 35 bottom left & right, 38, 40, 43 top & left), SportsChrome (10, 11, 35 top),
Topps, Inc. (15, 21, 28, 42 top and bottom left), Sportfolio (17), Macfadden Publications (24),
Bowman Gum Co. (25, 34 bottom right), SSPC (26), Exhibit Supply Co. (30, 45),
Cleveland Indians (33, 36), Sweet Caporal (34 bottom left),
The Helen Kuneman Loykovich Collection (34 top), TCMA, Ltd. (41), Matt Richman (48).
Cover Photo: Joe Robbins/Getty Images

The memorabilia and artifacts pictured in this book are presented for educational and informational purposes,
and come from the collection of the author.

Editor: Mike Kennedy
Designer: Ron Jaffe
Project Management: Black Book Partners, LLC.
Special thanks to Joan Loykovich.
Special thanks to Topps, Inc.

Library of Congress Cataloging-in-Publication Data

Stewart, Mark, 1960-
  The Cleveland Indians / by Mark Stewart.
      p. cm. -- (Team spirit)
  Includes bibliographical references and index.
  Summary: "A Team Spirit Baseball edition featuring the Cleveland Indians
that chronicles the history and accomplishments of the team. Includes access
to the Team Spirit website, which provides additional information, updates
and photos"--Provided by publisher.
  ISBN 978-1-59953-479-4 (library : alk. paper) -- ISBN 978-1-60357-359-7
(ebook) 1. Cleveland Indians (Baseball team)--History--Juvenile
literature. I. Title.
  GV875.C7S835 2012
  796.357'640977132--dc23
                                                          2011048172

Manufactured in the United States of America in North Mankato, Minnesota.
196N—012012

COVER PHOTO: The Indians can hardly wait to celebrate a 2011 win.

TABLE OF CONTENTS

ABOUT OUR GLOSSARY

In this book, there may be several words that you are reading for the first time. Some are sports words, some are new vocabulary words, and some are familiar words that are used in an unusual way. All of these words are defined on page 46. Throughout the book, sports words appear in **bold type**. Regular vocabulary words appear in ***bold italic type***.

MEET THE INDIANS

In most cities, going to a baseball game is just one of many things people like to do. In Cleveland, Ohio, watching the Indians is a way of life. Many of the people sitting in the ballpark or tuning in on television are part of families that have been rooting for the team for *generations*.

When the Indians are playing well, everyone in town has an extra hop in their step. If the team is playing for a championship, the entire state of Ohio comes alive with energy. Every winter, fans talk about the past season and make predictions about the season to come.

This book tells the story of the Indians. Whether they are up or down, in the running or out of it, the Indians are always a hot topic of conversation in Cleveland. That was true a century ago, and it will be the same way for many years to come.

Matt LaPorta gets a high-five from Jack Hannahan after a home run.

GLORY DAYS

The **American League (AL)** played its first season in 1901. Cleveland was one of the eight cities that got a team in the new league. The club was called the Blues. In 1902, they changed their name to the Bronchoes. A year later, they changed names again, this time to the Naps. They would not become the Indians for another 12 seasons.

The Naps were named in honor of Napoleon Lajoie, their best player. Lajoie was the AL's most popular star in those early years. His teammates included Joe Jackson, Cy Young, Addie Joss, Elmer Flick, and Bill Bradley. In 1908, the Naps fell one victory short of winning the **pennant**.

The Indians rose to the top of the AL in 1920 under **player-manager** Tris Speaker. The team had a great pitching staff that included Stan Coveleski, Jim Bagby, Slim Caldwell, and George Uhle. Cleveland won the **World Series** that fall and seemed to be headed for great things. But baseball was changing, and sluggers would soon rule the game. Cleveland could not find the power hitters it needed to challenge baseball's best teams.

Still, many more stars wore the Cleveland uniform during the 1920s and 1930s. Hal Trosky, Earl Averill, Joe Sewell, and Charlie Jamieson were among the AL's best hitters. Mel Harder, Willis Hudlin, and Bob Feller were among the top pitchers. No one in baseball had a fastball as good as Feller's. He arrived in Cleveland as a teenager and became the city's most popular player.

The Indians finally returned to the World Series in 1948. That team starred Feller and player-manager Lou Boudreau. They joined forces with Ken Keltner, Joe Gordon, Gene Bearden, Bob Lemon, and others to win the pennant in a thrilling **playoff** with the Boston

LEFT: Napoleon Lajoie poses for photographers.
ABOVE: Bob Feller tends to his mitt on the dugout steps.

Red Sox. One of Cleveland's best hitters was Larry Doby, the first African-American to play for an AL club.

The Indians had their greatest regular season in 1954, when they won 111 games. Lemon, Mike Garcia, and Early Wynn led the pitching staff. Doby, Al Rosen, and Al Smith powered the offense. Unfortunately, the Indians lost the World Series that fall. Still, Cleveland fans believed another championship would come soon.

Bad luck and bad trades haunted the Indians in the years that followed. In fact, it would be more than four **decades** before the fans got to celebrate another pennant. During that time, they cheered for stars such as Rocky Colavito, Sam McDowell, Luis Tiant, Buddy Bell, Andre Thornton, Julio Franco, and Joe Carter. But none of these players could lead Cleveland back to the World Series.

In the 1990s, the Indians finally put together a group of young stars ready to capture the pennant. Albert Belle, Jim Thome,

LEFT: Larry Doby warms up before a game.
ABOVE: Jim Thome watches a high fly ball leave his bat.

Omar Vizquel, Manny Ramirez, Carlos Baerga, and Kenny Lofton made up the heart of that team. The Indians signed these players to long contracts when they were young. Cleveland also added experienced pitchers Orel Hershiser and Dennis Martinez. In 1995 and again in 1997, the team went to the World Series.

The Indians finished first or second in the **AL Central** eight times in a row from 1994 to 2001, but they did not win a championship. Cleveland turned to a new group of players to get the club closer to this goal. Among the best were pitchers CC Sabathia, Cliff Lee, and Fausto Carmona. The Indians put together an explosive offense that included Travis Hafner, Victor Martinez, and Grady Sizemore. They helped Cleveland win another AL Central crown in 2007.

More good players worked their way into the Cleveland lineup in the years that followed. Some had played in the **minor leagues** for the Indians. Some came in trades from other teams. Young stars such as Michael Brantley, Carlos Santana, Asdrubal Cabrera, Matt LaPorta, Chris Perez, Josh Tomlin, and Justin Masterson gave fans hope that another championship was just around the corner. They helped the Indians become one of the most exciting teams in baseball.

LEFT: CC Sabathia delivers a pitch.
ABOVE: Grady Sizemore gives the ball a ride.

HOME TURF

F or more than 40 years, Cleveland's stadium was League Park. Originally, in the 1890s, it was home to a **National League (NL)** team called the Spiders. In 1901, the Indians (then known as the Blues) began playing there. In the 1930s, the Indians moved to Municipal Stadium. It was very big—and very cold when the wind whipped off Lake Erie. Some fans nicknamed it the "Mistake on the Lake."

In 1994, the Indians opened a spectacular new stadium. It was originally called Jacobs Field after team owners Richard and Dave Jacobs. It is a very modern building with a few touches to remind fans of Cleveland's history. The left field **bleachers** are extremely popular. A lot of home runs are hit there during batting practice.

BY THE NUMBERS

- The Indians' stadium has 43,441 seats.
- The distance from home plate to the left field foul pole is 325 feet.
- The distance from home plate to the center field fence is 405 feet.
- The distance from home plate to the right field foul pole is 325 feet.

Fans in Cleveland watch the Indians during a playoff game in 2007.

Early in their history, the Indians used navy blue and white as their team colors. In 1916, each player wore a number on his sleeve. That was the first time a big-league team featured uniform numbers. A year later, the numbers were removed.

The Indians added red to their uniforms in the 1930s. In the 1960s, the team wore sleeveless jerseys with bright red caps. For a few years in the 1970s, the Indians wore road uniforms with red tops and red pants. In 2011, the team introduced new uniforms with an old-time feel to them.

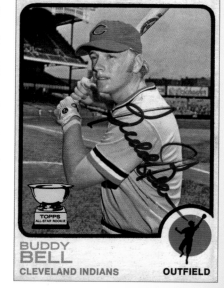

BUDDY BELL
CLEVELAND INDIANS   **OUTFIELD**

The team's *logo* shows a Native American cartoon character nicknamed "Chief Wahoo." The Indians have been using him since the 1940s. Some fans have argued that Chief Wahoo is disrespectful to Native Americans. The team disagrees with them and is proud of its name.

LEFT: Asdrubal Cabrera wears the team's 2011 road uniform.
ABOVE: Buddy Bell poses in the team's road uniform from the early 1970s.

WE WON!

The Indians played 99 seasons during the 20th century. They won four pennants and the World Series twice. The team's first championship came at a great cost. Ray Chapman, the city's most beloved player, was hit in the head with a pitch during an August game and died. Those were the days before players wore batting helmets. Chapman's replacement, a **rookie** named Joe Sewell, helped the Indians win the pennant. He went on to enter the **Hall of Fame**.

The Indians met the Brooklyn Robins in the 1920 World Series. The first team to win five games would be the champion. Cleveland had very good pitching, including starters Jim Bagby and Stan Coveleski. After falling behind Brooklyn two games to one, the Indians took the next four games in a row. Coveleski won three games. Cleveland catcher Steve O'Neill batted .333 during the series and handled the team's pitchers perfectly.

In 1948, the Indians finished the season tied with the Boston Red Sox. A one-game playoff would decide the pennant winner. The teams met in Boston's Fenway Park. Lou Boudreau, the AL **Most Valuable Player (MVP)** that year, smashed two home runs for the Indians, who won 8–3.

The Indians did not have to travel far for the World Series. They faced the Boston Braves, who played just across town. The experts picked the Indians to win. They had three terrific pitchers—Bob Feller,

Bob Lemon, and Gene Bearden. The Braves had only two pitching stars, Warren Spahn and Johnny Sain.

Cleveland took three of the first four games thanks to great pitching and timely hitting. Larry Doby made history with the winning home run in Game 4. It was the first homer hit in the World Series by an African-American player. The Braves' hitters broke through in Game 5 with an 11–5 victory. Satchel Paige pitched in this game for the Indians. He was the first African-American pitcher to appear

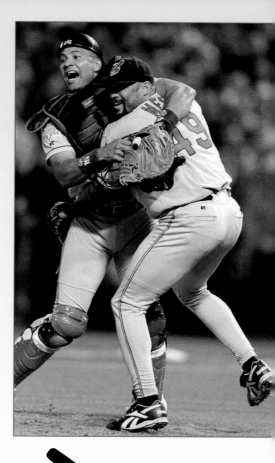

in a World Series. The next day, Lemon beat Boston 4–3 to win the championship.

The Indians won the pennant in 1954 but lost the World Series. In 1960, they traded Rocky Colavito, their best and most popular player. The Indians did not finish higher than third place for the next 34 seasons. Frustrated Cleveland fans called this streak the "Curse of Colavito."

The Indians finally won another pennant in 1995. Unfortunately, they lost the World Series to the Atlanta Braves. Two years later, Cleveland took the league championship again. They played the Florida Marlins in the World Series. With Cleveland three outs away from the championship, the Marlins tied the game and then won it in the 10th inning. Was it bad luck, bad timing, or the dreaded curse? No one knows for sure!

19

GO-TO GUYS

To be a true star in baseball, you need more than a quick bat and a strong arm. You have to be a "go-to guy"—someone the manager wants on the pitcher's mound or in the batter's box when it matters most. Fans of the Indians have had a lot to cheer about over the years, including these great stars ...

THE PIONEERS

NAPOLEON LAJOIE   Second Baseman

• BORN: 9/5/1874   • DIED: 2/7/1959   • PLAYED FOR TEAM: 1902 TO 1914

Napoleon Lajoie was a great hitter and fielder. He led the league in batting twice for the Indians. Fans adored Lajoie. In fact, he was so popular that the team was called the "Naps" when he played for Cleveland.

BOB FELLER   Pitcher

• BORN: 11/3/1918   • DIED: 12/15/2010
• PLAYED FOR TEAM: 1936 TO 1941 & 1945 TO 1956

Bob Feller threw harder than anyone in the 1930s and 1940s. He pitched three **no-hitters** and won 266 games. Feller would have won even more had he not served in the military during *World War II.*

RIGHT: Al Rosen

LOU BOUDREAU   Shortstop

• BORN: 7/17/1917   • DIED: 8/10/2001   • PLAYED FOR TEAM: 1938 TO 1950

Lou Boudreau was just 24 years old when he was named player-manager of the Indians in 1942. He was the league's top hitter in 1944 and led the Indians to the pennant in 1948.

BOB LEMON   Pitcher

• BORN: 9/22/1920   • DIED: 1/11/2000

• PLAYED FOR TEAM: 1941 TO 1942 & 1946 TO 1958

Bob Lemon played two years as an outfielder for Cleveland before becoming a pitcher. He was an All-Star seven times in a row. In 1948, Lemon won 20 games—including 10 by **shutout**!

LARRY DOBY   Outfielder

• BORN: 12/13/1923   • DIED: 6/18/2003

• PLAYED FOR TEAM: 1947 TO 1955 & 1958

Larry Doby was the best center fielder in the AL in the early 1950s. He was also a good hitter under pressure. Doby played in the **All-Star Game** seven times as a member of the Indians.

AL ROSEN   Third Baseman

• BORN: 2/29/1924

• PLAYED FOR TEAM: 1947 TO 1956

Al Rosen had one of the greatest seasons ever by a third baseman in 1953. He led the AL with 43 home runs and 145 RBIs. Rosen also hit .336 but lost the batting championship by one point.

JIM THOME   First Baseman/Third Baseman

- **BORN:** 8/27/1970   • **PLAYED FOR TEAM:** 1991 TO 2002 & 2011

Jim Thome was one of the most popular athletes ever to play in Cleveland. He powered the Indians to two pennants and was the league's most dangerous slugger in 2001 and 2002. During those two seasons, he slammed 101 home runs.

OMAR VIZQUEL   Shortstop

- **BORN:** 4/24/1967

- **PLAYED FOR TEAM:** 1994 TO 2004

Omar Vizquel was an amazing fielder who made the hard plays look easy. In the three seasons Vizquel played across from second baseman Roberto Alomar in Cleveland, they both won **Gold Gloves** each year.

ALBERT BELLE   Outfielder

- **BORN:** 8/25/1966

- **PLAYED FOR TEAM:** 1989 TO 1996

Once the Indians made Albert Belle an everyday player, he became one of baseball's most feared hitters. In 1995, Belle set a record by hitting 50 doubles and 50 home runs in the same season. The following year, he topped the AL with 148 **runs batted in (RBIs)**.

ASDRUBAL CABRERA Shortstop

- BORN: 11/13/1985 • FIRST YEAR WITH TEAM: 2007

The Indians traded for Asdrubal Carbera because of his defense. He rewarded them by making an unassisted triple play in 2008. In 2011, Cabrera surprised the team by hitting 25 home runs.

CC SABATHIA Pitcher

- BORN: 7/21/1980 • PLAYED FOR TEAM: 2001 TO 2008

CC Sabathia was the youngest player in baseball when he led the Indians to the **playoffs** in 2001. In 2007, he led them back to the playoffs and won the **Cy Young Award**.

CARLOS SANTANA Catcher

- BORN: 4/8/1986
- FIRST YEAR WITH TEAM: 2010

A championship team needs a smart and talented catcher. Carlos Santana showed he was that kind of player in just his second season. He did a good job with the team's young pitchers and became a dangerous power hitter, with 27 home runs and 35 doubles.

LEFT: Omar Vizquel
RIGHT: Carlos Santana

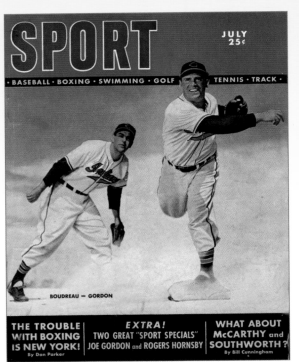

In the early days of baseball, it was common for clubs to ask their best players to also manage the team. Owners believed that their stars commanded the respect of their teammates. Sometimes this *strategy* worked, and sometimes it did not. The Indians had very good luck with player-managers.

Under Napoleon Lajoie, Cleveland was one of the top teams in the AL during the early 1900s. Tris Speaker managed the Indians to a World Series championship in his first full year in charge, in 1920. Lou Boudreau not only won a pennant as Cleveland's player-manager in 1948. He was also named the league MVP. In 1975, the Indians named Frank Robinson as their player-manager. He was the first African-American to manage a big-league club.

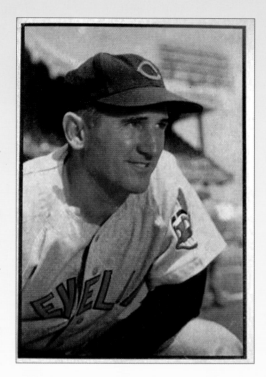

Cleveland's most successful manager was Al Lopez. Lopez had been an All-Star catcher in the 1930s and 1940s. His playing days were over when he came to the Indians in 1951, but he knew how to put together a great pitching staff. Many thought Lopez was a genius, but he gave all the credit to his players. In six seasons, he led the Indians to 90 or more victories five times. In 1954, Cleveland went 111–43.

The manager who guided Cleveland to the most first-place finishes was Mike Hargrove. As a player, Hargrove always seemed nervous. As a manager, he was very relaxed. When Hargrove took over the Indians in 1994, they were in last place. A year later, Cleveland won the AL Central. It marked the first time since 1954 that the team had finished first. Under Hargrove, the Indians finished atop the standings again each year from 1996 to 1999.

APRIL 8, 1975

On Opening Day in 1947, Jackie Robinson broke baseball's "color barrier." It took another 28 years before an African-American was hired to manage a big-league team. Frank Robinson joined the Indians at the end of the 1974 season and was named manager for Opening Day in 1975.

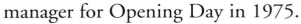

At the time, Robinson was nearing the end of his career as a player. He had more than 500 home runs to his credit and two MVP awards in his trophy case. His plan was to play in a few games for the Indians as a designated hitter. For Cleveland's first game of 1975, Robinson put his name on the lineup card.

That day, the Indians played the New York Yankees in Cleveland. The crowd of 57,000 gave Robinson a standing ovation as he walked toward home plate in the

first inning. Doc Medich threw two good pitches, and Robinson took them both for strikes. He fouled off the third pitch and took the next two for balls.

Medich's next delivery was low and on the outside part of home plate. Robinson reached out and met the pitch with a smooth swing. The ball soared high to left field and sailed over the fence. It was the 575th home run of Robinson's career. As he circled the bases, the entire team came out to meet him. "I'm living my biggest moment in baseball," Robinson thought to himself.

Robinson did a good job in his first year. The Indians had their first winning record since 1968. Those who predicted he would be a good manager were correct—Robinson was still managing in the majors more than 30 years later!

LEGEND HAS IT

WERE THE INDIANS NAMED AFTER LOUIS SOCKALEXIS?

LEGEND HAS IT that they were. However, this may only be a legend. Sockalexis was a Native American who played for the Cleveland Spiders in the 1800s. The Spiders went out of business, but the fans still remembered Sockalexis. When the team held a contest in 1915 to find a new name, the winning choice was Indians. Was this to honor Sockalexis, or because a team called the Braves had recently won a World Series championship? No one will ever know for sure.

ABOVE: Topps printed this trading card of Louis Sockalexis more than a century after he played.

WHICH INDIAN CAUGHT BIG AIR?

LEGEND HAS IT that Jim Thome did. No, Thome wasn't a skateboarder. But almost half the time he came to the plate, he did not hit the ball—he either walked or struck out. In 1999, Thome led the AL with 127 walks and 171 strikeouts. The last American Leaguer to top the league in both categories was Mickey Mantle, in 1958. Thome was a patient hitter. If he didn't get a pitch he liked, he was happy to take four balls and trot down to first base. When he did swing, he swung hard— and often missed the ball entirely. Of course, when he hit one, it left his bat like a rocket!

WHICH CLEVELAND STAR WON HIS BATTLE AGAINST A CRIPPLING DISEASE CALLED POLIO?

LEGEND HAS IT that Vic Wertz did. Wertz helped the Indians win 111 games in 1954. In 1955, doctors told him that his career might be over. He had polio, a disease that attacks the muscles. Many victims of polio became paralyzed. Wertz recovered and played in 74 games for the Indians that summer. In 1956, he hit 32 home runs and tied a record with four doubles in a game.

Baseball fans love it when they go to a game and see something no one has ever seen before. The fans who bought tickets to Game 5 of the 1920 World Series definitely got their money's worth.

Elmer Smith
OUTFIELDER

The Indians and Brooklyn Robins split the first four games. As the fifth game began, the fans in Cleveland settled into their seats for a battle between hometown favorite Jim Bagby and Brooklyn's Burleigh Grimes. They were two of the best pitchers in baseball.

The Indians struck first, in the bottom of the first inning. They loaded the bases for Elmer Smith, who hit a pitch over the right field fence. It was the first grand slam in the history of the World Series. Three innings later, Bagby hit another home run for Cleveland. It was the first long ball by a pitcher in the World Series.

LEFT: Elmer Smith's home run gave the Indians an early lead in Game 5. **RIGHT**: Bill Wambsganss made history in the 1920 World Series with an unassisted triple play.

The Indians had more surprises in store for the fans. In the fifth inning, Clarence Mitchell came to bat for Brooklyn with two men on and no one out. Mitchell lined a pitch up the middle. Second baseman, Bill Wambsganss—known to everyone as "Wamby"—darted to his right and speared the ball out of the air. He stepped on second base before the runner could get back for a double play.

Wambsganss then turned and saw Otto Miller, who was running from first base. Miller thought the ball had made it to the outfield. He was in shock when Wambsganss tagged him for the third out. It was the first—and only—unassisted triple play in World Series history.

The stunned Robins did not recover. The Indians surrendered only one run in the next 22 innings and won their first World Series.

TEAM SPIRIT

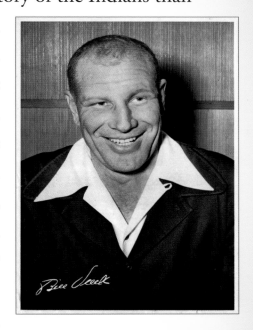

No one had more team spirit in the history of the Indians than Bill Veeck. He bought the club in 1946. Under Veeck's ownership, Cleveland hired bands and performers to roam the stands. Races were held on the field between games of doubleheaders. The Indians were one of the first teams to shoot off fireworks, too. Once, a fan named Joe Early wrote a letter to the team saying Cleveland should honor its fans. What did the Indians do? They held Joe Early Night!

Today the team continues this *tradition*. Every season, the Indians have special giveaway days and other *promotions*. Indeed, there is a lot to do at the Cleveland ballpark. That includes watching and playing with Slider, the team's pink, furry mascot.

LEFT: Slider joins the Indians as they listen to the national anthem.
ABOVE: Bill Veeck always had fun ideas for the fans.

TIMELINE

This ticket is from the first game at Municipal Stadium.

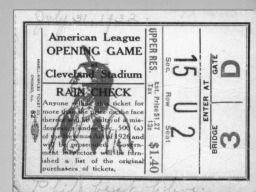

1920
The Indians win the World Series.

1932
Municipal Stadium opens in Cleveland.

1901
The team plays its first season.

1941
Jeff Heath becomes the first AL player to hit 20 doubles, triples, and homers in the same season.

1954
The Indians win 111 games and reach their third World Series.

Bill Bradley played third base for the 1901 team.

Larry Doby led the AL in homers and RBIs in 1954.

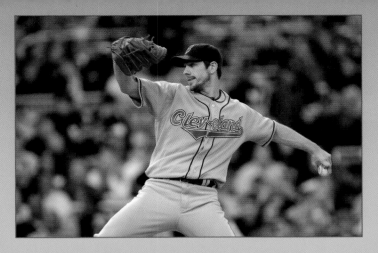

Cliff
Lee

1995

The Indians win their
first pennant in 41 years.

2008

Cliff Lee wins the
Cy Young Award.

1986

Joe Carter leads
the AL with
121 RBIs.

1999

Manny Ramirez drives in
165 runs—the most by a
player in more than 60 years.

2010

Shin-Soo Choo
hits three homers
in one game.

Joe
Carter

Shin-Soo
Choo

Fun Facts

What Might Have Been

Herb Score won 36 games and struck out 508 batters in his first two seasons for Cleveland. In 1958, he was hit in the eye by a line drive and was never the same pitcher again.

Old Satch

No one was sure how old Satchel Paige was when he made his first big-league start for the Indians in 1948. Paige proved age didn't matter when he pitched a shutout against the Chicago White Sox.

Try Harder

As a player for the Indians in the 1930s and 1940s, Mel Harder had helped teammates Bob Feller and Bob Lemon become top pitchers. After Harder retired, Cleveland made him baseball's first full-time pitching coach.

ABOVE: Satchel Paige

TALL ORDER

In 1938, the Indians set a weird world record. Third baseman Ken Keltner went to the top of Cleveland's 708-foot Terminal Tower and dropped baseballs to teammates Frank Pytlak and Hank Helf. After a few misses, they became the first players to catch baseballs dropped from more than 700 feet.

RECORD BREAKER

When Jim Thome hit 49 home runs in 2001, he broke Hal Trosky's team record for lefties. When he hit 52 a year later, he beat Albert Belle's team record of 50.

AND ... ACTION

Harry Bay and Napoleon Lajoie were the first baseball players to appear in a movie. Both were filmed after the 1903 season. Several Indians were also in the 1949 film "The Kid from Cleveland."

STAR POWER

During the early 1900s, Cleveland's Elmer Flick was rated as one of the best all-around players in the AL. The Detroit Tigers liked Flick so much that they once offered Ty Cobb in a trade for him.

TALKING BASEBALL

"This is the place I want to play for a very long time. I pretty much love everything about the Indians."

▶ **TRAVIS HAFNER**, ON PLAYING IN CLEVELAND

"I sign every autograph I can for kids because I remember myself at that age."

▶ **JIM THOME**, ON HOW HE GIVES BACK TO THE FANS

"The baselines belong to the runner, and whenever I was running the bases, I always slid hard. "

▶ **FRANK ROBINSON**, ON GIVING 100 PERCENT ON THE BASE PATHS

"I would rather beat the Yankees regularly than pitch a no-hit game."

▶ **BOB FELLER**, ON HIS BIGGEST PERSONAL RIVAL

"A pitcher's got to be good and he's got to be lucky."

▶ **CY YOUNG**, ON WHAT IT TAKES TO BE A SUCCESSFUL BIG-LEAGUE PITCHER

"I knew being accepted was going to be hard, but I knew I was involved in a situation that was going to bring opportunities to other blacks."

▶ **LARY DOBY**, ON BEING THE FIRST AFRICAN-AMERICAN TO PLAY IN THE AL

"When you're a manager, all the worries of the team become your worries."

▶ **AL LOPEZ**, ON THE RESPONSIBILITY OF MANAGING

LEFT: Travis Hafner   **ABOVE**: Bob Feller meets Cy Young many years after Young pitched for the Indians.

GREAT DEBATES

People who root for the Indians love to compare their favorite moments, teams, and players. Some debates have been going on for years! How would you settle these classic baseball arguments?

IN 1995, ALBERT BELLE HAD THE MOST AMAZING SEASON OF ANY INDIAN ...

… because he led the AL in runs, RBIs, doubles, and home runs. Basically, Belle (LEFT) just crushed the ball all year long. He had 52 doubles and 50 homers. That means more than 100 times he either ended up on second after a hit—or circled the bases. No one had ever had a "50-50" season before. And Belle did it in only 143 games!

LOU BOUDREAU'S 1948 SEASON IS THE DEFINITION OF AMAZING ...

… because he won the AL MVP and managed the Indians to their second championship. Boudreau hit .355, scored 116 runs, and drove in 106. As Cleveland's leader in the dugout, he guided the team to a record of 104–51 for the pennant. In the World Series, he topped all hitters with four doubles, as the Indians beat the Boston Braves in six games.

CC SABATHIA WAS THE INDIANS' FINEST LEFT-HANDED PITCHER …

… because he was getting big-league batters out when most pitchers his age were still in the minor leagues. Sabathia was the youngest player in baseball in 2001, but he threw like a pitcher with great experience. He went 17–5 that season and led the Indians to the playoffs. Sabathia got better and better after that. He won his 100th game at the age of 27 and captured the Cy Young Award as the league's top pitcher in 2007.

ARE YOU SURE? SOME SAY SAM MCDOWELL WAS THE MOST UNHITTABLE LEFTY THEY EVER SAW …

… because from 1965 to 1970, he led the AL in strikeouts five times. McDowell (RIGHT) was nicknamed "Sudden Sam" because his pitching motion looked so relaxed—and then suddenly the ball popped into the catcher's mitt. He threw very hard, but he was also a little wild. That kept batters from getting comfortable at home plate. When McDowell was on his game, he was almost impossible to hit. In most games, he had more strikeouts than hits.

FOR THE RECORD

The great Indians teams and players have left their marks on the record books. These are the "best of the best" …

Gaylord Perry

Andre Thornton

INDIANS AWARD WINNERS

WINNER	AWARD	YEAR
Lou Boudreau	Most Valuable Player	1948
Al Rosen	Most Valuable Player	1953
Herb Score	Rookie of the Year*	1955
Chris Chambliss	Rookie of the Year	1971
Gaylord Perry	Cy Young Award	1972
Boog Powell	Comeback Player of the Year	1975
Joe Charboneau	Rookie of the Year	1980
Andre Thornton	Comeback Player of the Year	1982
Sandy Alomar Jr.	Rookie of the Year	1990
David Justice	Comeback Player of the Year	1997
Sandy Alomar Jr.	All-Star Game MVP	1997
CC Sabathia	Cy Young Award	2007
Eric Wedge	Manager of the Year	2007
Cliff Lee	Cy Young Award	2008
Cliff Lee	Comeback Player of the Year	2008

Rookie of the Year—The annual award given to each league's best first-year player.

Fans bought this pennant during the 1920 season.

INDIANS ACHIEVEMENTS

ACHIEVEMENT	YEAR
AL Pennant Winners	1920
World Series Champions	1920
AL Pennant Winners	1948
World Series Champions	1948
AL Pennant Winners	1954
AL Central Champions	1995
AL Pennant Winners	1995
AL Central Champions	1996
AL Central Champions	1997
AL Pennant Winners	1997
AL Central Champions	1998
AL Central Champions	1999
AL Central Champions	2001
AL Central Champions	2007

ABOVE: Herb Score was the Rookie of the Year in 1955.
LEFT: Kenny Lofton led the AL in triples and steals in 1995.
BELOW: Fans wore this souvenir pin of the 1954 team.

CLEVELAND INDIANS
1954
AMERICAN LEAGUE CHAMPIONS

43

PINPOINTS

T he history of a baseball team is made up of many smaller stories. These stories take place all over the map—not just in the city a team calls "home." Match the pushpins on these maps to the **TEAM FACTS**, and you will begin to see the story of the Indians unfold!

TEAM FACTS

1. Cleveland, Ohio—*The Indians have played here since 1901.*
2. Van Meter, Iowa—*Bob Feller was born here.*
3. Jamestown, North Dakota—*Travis Hafner was born here.*
4. Miami, Florida—*The Indians played in the 1997 World Series here.*
5. Shreveport, Louisiana—*Albert Belle was born here.*
6. Spartanburg, South Carolina—*Al Rosen was born here.*
7. Tuskegee, Alabama—*Andre Thornton was born here.*
8. Boston, Massachusetts—*The Indians won the 1948 World Series here.*
9. San Bernardino, California—*Bob Lemon was born here.*
10. Snohomish, Washington—*Earl Averill was born here.*
11. Hato Mayor, Dominican Republic—*Julio Franco was born here.*
12. Caracas, Venezuela—*Omar Vizquel was born here.*

Bob Lemon

GLOSSARY

BASEBALL WORDS
VOCABULARY WORDS

AL CENTRAL—A group of American League teams that play in the central part of the country.

ALL-STAR GAME—Baseball's annual game featuring the best players from the American League and National League.

AMERICAN LEAGUE (AL)—One of baseball's two major leagues; the AL began play in 1901.

BLEACHERS—The unprotected seats located in the outfield, where fans get "bleached" by the sun.

CY YOUNG AWARD—The award given each year to each league's best pitcher.

DECADES—Periods of 10 years; also specific periods, such as the 1950s.

GENERATIONS—Periods of years roughly equal to the time it takes for a person to be born, grow up, and have children.

GOLD GLOVES—The awards given each year to baseball's best fielders.

HALL OF FAME—The museum in Cooperstown, New York, where baseball's greatest players are honored.

LOGO—A symbol or design that represents a company or team.

MINOR LEAGUES—The many professional leagues that help develop players for the major leagues.

MOST VALUABLE PLAYER (MVP)—The award given each year to each league's top player; an MVP is also selected for the World Series and the All-Star Game.

NATIONAL LEAGUE (NL)—The older of the two major leagues; the NL began play in 1876.

NO-HITTERS—Games in which a team does not get a hit.

PENNANT—A league championship. The term comes from the triangular flag awarded to each season's champion, beginning in the 1870s.

PLAYER-MANAGER—A player who also manages his team.

PLAYOFF—A game that helps determine who will play for a championship. A special one-game playoff is used to break a tie at the end of the regular season.

PLAYOFFS—The games played after the regular season to determine which teams will advance to the World Series.

PROMOTIONS—Fun events and programs for fans.

ROOKIE—A player in his first season.

RUNS BATTED IN (RBIs)—A statistic that counts the number of runners a batter drives home.

SHUTOUT—A game in which one team does not score a run.

STRATEGY—A plan or method for succeeding.

TRADITION—A belief or custom that is handed down from generation to generation.

WORLD SERIES—The world championship series played between the AL and NL pennant winners.

WORLD WAR II—The war between the major powers of Europe, Asia, and North America that lasted from 1939 to 1945. The United States entered the war in 1941.

EXTRA INNINGS

TEAM SPIRIT introduces a great way to stay up to date with your team! Visit our **EXTRA INNINGS** link and get connected to the latest and greatest updates. **EXTRA INNINGS** serves as a young reader's ticket to an exclusive web page—with more stories, fun facts, team records, and photos of the Indians. Content is updated during and after each season. The **EXTRA INNINGS** feature also enables readers to send comments and letters to the author! Log onto:

www.norwoodhousepress.com/library.aspx

and click on the tab: **TEAM SPIRIT** to access **EXTRA INNINGS**.

Read all the books in the series to learn more about professional sports. For a complete listing of the baseball, basketball, football, and hockey teams in the **TEAM SPIRIT** series, visit our website at:

www.norwoodhousepress.com/library.aspx

ON THE ROAD

CLEVELAND INDIANS
2401 Ontario Street
Cleveland, Ohio 44115
(216) 420-4487
cleveland.indians.mlb.com

**NATIONAL BASEBALL
HALL OF FAME AND MUSEUM**
25 Main Street
Cooperstown, New York 13326
(888) 425-5633
www.baseballhalloffame.org

ON THE BOOKSHELF

To learn more about the sport of baseball, look for these books at your library or bookstore:

- Augustyn, Adam (editor). *The Britannica Guide to Baseball*. New York, NY: Rosen Publishing, 2011.

- Dreier, David. *Baseball: How It Works*. North Mankato, MN: Capstone Press, 2010.

- Stewart, Mark. *Ultimate 10: Baseball*. New York, NY: Gareth Stevens Publishing, 2009.

INDEX

ABOUT THE AUTHOR

MARK STEWART has written more than 50 books on baseball and over 150 sports books for kids. He grew up in New York City during the 1960s rooting for the Yankees and Mets, and was lucky enough to meet players from both teams. Mark comes from a family of writers. His grandfather was Sunday Editor of *The New York Times,* and his mother was Articles Editor of *Ladies' Home Journal* and *McCall's.* Mark has profiled hundreds of athletes over the past 25 years. He has also written several books about his native New York and New Jersey, his home today. Mark is a graduate of Duke University, with a degree in history. He lives and works in a home overlooking Sandy Hook, New Jersey. You can contact Mark through the Norwood House Press website.